EVERYTHING IN BETWEEN

EVERYTHING IN BETWEEN

Poems That Reflect Life's Deepest Echos

DONALD K. BINGHAM

DEDICATION

To the wanderers who find beauty in the spaces between moments and dreams. To the storytellers who pour their hearts into words and the listeners who find joy in their rhythm.

This compilation is for those moments of searching—for unity, for shared experiences, for the quiet truths whispered in the dark and the dreams that take flight when the world slows down.

To my family and friends—thank you for your love and support. You've been my rock through it all, and I couldn't have done this without you.

And to you, the reader—thank you for picking up this book and stepping into these pages. It means the world that you're here, sharing in these words with me. I hope you find a part of your own story in these lines, something that speaks to you and lingers in your heart.

INTRODUCTION

Step into *Everything In Between*, a collection of poetry that weaves together themes of love, loss, faith, and social justice. These poems explore the deeply human moments we all experience—the vulnerability, the resilience, and the hope that shape our lives.

Through each verse, you'll feel the tender highs of love, the quiet ache of loss, the steady light of faith, and the unshakable drive to stand for what's right. This treasure trove of poems invites you to pause, reflect, and find comfort or inspiration in life's complexities.

Everything In Between is more than just a book of poetry—it's a celebration of the beauty and strength found in our shared struggles and victories. Perfect for those who long to feel deeply, connect meaningfully, and rediscover their own inner strength.

TABLE OF CONTENTS

DEDICATION5	V
INTRODUCTION	VII
CHAPTER 1: Threads Of Passion	1
Treasures Of The Heart	2
To Whome It May Concern	4
Naughty Girl	6
In Dout	8
Echos Of Love	10
Karaoke Night	12
Lingering Love	14
Star Dust	16
Unger The Moonlight	17
Burn It All	18
A Symphony Of Love	20
Heartache	21
What's Good	22
I Found You	23
If This Is Love	24
If I Could	26
Girl Tonight	28
CHAPTER 2: Minutes And Memories	29
Petals & Thorns	30
17 Floors	32
Mother Earth	34
Happy Hour	36
Sunshine & Joy	37
Tin Roof	38
If Not Me	40
Bitters Tears	41
I'm Home	42
Anywhere But Here	44
CHAPTER 3: Beyond The Veil	45
Faith Endures	46
My Guarden	48
Broken Wings	49
Phantom Whispers	50
Love Immortal	51

TABLE OF CONTENTS

Eternal Trust	52
Cycle Of Life	53
God' Signature	54
Reflections	55
Eden's First Tale	56
My Saving Grace	58
CHAPTER 4: Fight For Tomorrow	**59**
Fight For Tomorrow	59
Black Swan	60
Brown Face	62
The Eagle Soars	63
Black Excellence	64
Black Face	66
The Stigma	67
Greed Of The Man	68
In The Ghetto	70
Rich Eat Poor	72
A Colony	74
Slave Progeny	76
Democracy?	78
This Old Thing	79
I Was There	80
No Escaping The Past	82
Endnote	83
About The Author	85

CHAPTER 1

THREADS OF PASSION

The invisible thread of love that runs through us all, stitching together moments that make life real. Love doesn't just shape our lives—it leaves fingerprints on who we are.

These poems hold the rush of a first kiss, the ache of letting someone go, and the unspoken hope that lingers in the aftermath. They're about the beauty of togetherness, the courage it takes to stay when things get hard, and the strength we discover when love asks us to stand on our own.

Whether you're just beginning to discover love or finding your way back to yourself after loss, this section is a celebration of love's power—not just to shape us or break us, but to remind us what it means to truly live.

TREASURES OF THE HEART

Echoes of intent to love,
Love you, I will.
No diamonds in the rough
Can compare to my Love.
Love I freely give.

Every drop of rain I'd rescind,
Craft for you the bluest sky.
Whisper to the winds,
To carry my intent far and wide.

Beneath the morning sun,
The radiance of Love unfurls;
No wind, nor rain, or winter's
Cold can break our bond.

To the infinite beyond
My heart to you belong,
Prince or vagabond,
My heart for you a throne.

Your name is my song.
I'd enlist the songbirds
In the trees, to compose a
Symphony for you alone,

Place at your feet riches untold,
The moon to adorn as a crown,
Gilded streets for you to stroll,
My generosity knows no bounds.

Smitten by your smile,
The shape of your eyes,
Skin kissed by the sun.
Your lips, I so desired,
I want this wish with all
The aches this tender heart.

Love you, I will.
No diamonds in the rough
Can compare to my Love.
Love I freely give.

TO WHOME IT MAY CONCERN

So much time has passed since I saw you last,
And I'm not sure how to feel about that.
When we last spoke, It ended on a sour note.
I believe you called me out of my name.

My ears hung on every word, trying to
Understand by reason alone.
Loves, a word better felt than heard—
But now those feelings are all gone.

I went missing—withdrawn,
All caught up in my feels.
I all but disappeared.
Even holidays hit different.
The worst time Of the year
For me, is Christmas.

That's around the time we first met,
Snowflake and Mistletoe.
How can I ever forget?
Even now, I smile—just a
Little bit.
You see that's the problem,
I would if I could, forget.
But I'm just left to wonder—
Sometimes, I wish we never met.

TO WHOME IT MAY CONCERN

We never kissed—never laughed, and—
you know—Did-it.

I saved your pictures on my phone
So I wouldn't have to be alone.

These feelings shadow my waking day.
I mean, look at you—blocking all my calls.
How is it so easy for you to walk away,
To move on?

Hopefully, this will be the last letter
I write— "To Whom It May Concern."

Hopefully, this time next year
I, too, would have moved on—

Merry Christmas!

NAUGHTY GIRL

We meet every June
Before the harvest moon
When Love is a naughty girl.

Tonight, her flower blooms,
She emerges from her cocoon
As the radiant world unfurls.

Standing under the glow
Her silhouette strikes a pose,
Nimble fingers beckon.

Soft winds caress her body
The gale, playful and loddy,
A feeling as surreal as Heaven.

This dance is a ritual
Up on her tiptoes
I then lean in for a kiss—
And it is sweet.

All night, skin-to-skin,
Our souls together blend,
Beautiful mahogany.

From her well, I took a sip,
Liquids dripped from my lips
Down below her navel,

NAUGHTY GIRL

Fingertips they grip,
Supple thighs and hips,
Then, slowly, I let go.

Bodies dance, telling a story
Spoken-Word type poetry
Beneath the ebb and flow.

She's an angel in disguise
Gone before sunrise
Her beauty is a work of art.

We have a moment together,
But, like good and bad weather,
We divide and then flow wide apart.

IN DOUBT

When in the night
The stars begin to gleam,
And silence wraps the earth
In a soft embrace,
I find within your eyes
A shining beam,
A love that time and space
Can never erase.

Through seasons' change
And fortune's cruel caprice,
Your steadfast heart remains
My guiding light.

No tempest fierce nor
Tempest's roaring peace
Could shake the bond we
Forged in the darkest night.

When the frailness of beauty
Dare not show it's face
When the strength of youth
And I have parted ways,
In love, we'll find delight.

IN DOUBT

So let the winds untamed
Blow fierce and wild,
And let the tides of fate
Their courses chart.

For in your gaze,
Forever reconciled,
I find the refuge of
A loving heart.

Together, we shall stand,
Come joy or sorrow,
And face each dawn as one,
Through each tomorrow.

ECHOS OF LOVE

Empty picture frames
In my bedroom hang,
Sometimes I stop and stare.

Cherished memories
Fill the vacancy,
Then, slowly disappear.

In this empty room,
Lingering perfume
That you used to wear,

Reminds me of your touch,
I reach out for what
It is no longer there.

My world, now a little off-beat,
No rhythm in my feet,
Now that you're not here.

I try to compose a melody,
The tinkling of piano keys,
Puts me in my feels.

ECHOS OF LOVE

Echos of love stain the walls
In this room—that room,
Even down the hall.

Confronted by what we had
The Ghost of Lover's Past
It keeps me up at night.

This space, a mourner's,
Love lingers in every corner,
A vision of what used to be.

In the silence of your absence.
Echoes of your laughter,
Now, a bittersweet symphony.

KARAOKE NIGHT

In this room, there are many.
They dance to sing-a-longs.
Conversing is plenty
Communion wasn't in me
So, I decided to write a poem,

About a girl I once knew,
Who loved to sing the blues,
She left me in search of fame.

The world I would roam,
To watch her sing her songs,
She was always glad I came.

She'd put me in a trance,
Beneath lights that danced,
Like the stars above.

Every word, every note,
Each syllable from her throat,
 A story told with love.

This went on for years,
Until the urge disappeared
Wandering hearts that roamed.

KARAOKE NIGHT

I was there—the last show,
Lights dimmed, curtains closed,
The microphone dropped.

She grew old, and so did I
I had never seen her cry
And for a while she never stopped.

Today, her life is simple.
 But not even a few wrinkles,
Could keep her off the grid.

It's karaoke night—
Beneath the spotlight
Again in the center ring,

There's one of pure delight,
My friend—my wife,
And man, she can still sing.

LINGERING LOVE

If I never told you,
You mean the world to me;
It would be untrue,
Like stories written in books,
Forgotten tales of love and loss.

Without you, it's hard to breathe.
Every breath is a struggle;
You said forever we,
Promised eternal togetherness.
Forever means never to leave,
But here I am, alone, clinging to
Memories—

My girl, the magician, shrouded
In mystery
Casting spells of love and confusion,
You got me hoping and wishing,
Caught in the web of your enigma.
For now, the mystery is: will you ever
Return or at least tell me what it is,
That I've done?

Why did you plant a seed?
A seed of hope in barren soil,
I still want to believe in the
Possibility of us.

LINGERING LOVE

Hold me down like gravity,
Rooted in the place of shared
Dreams—now drifting apart.
Hello, are you still there?

I'm crying out to lovers past,
Echoes of ancient romance;
I want to know, do you still care
About the love we once shared?

I know it's so unfair;
Life's cruel twists and turns,
Never a doubt, in my mind,
The incredible love we had,
Moments etched in time.

I know girls can be players too—
Please tell me that's not you.
That's not what this is about.
Hello, are you still there?

In the shadows of memories,
In the whisper of the wind,
In the silence of the night,
I search for signs of you.
Longing for a connection,
Hoping for your response,
To this endless question—
Are you still there?

STAR DUST

Stranded in time,
Somewhere in outer space.
Wondrous sublime,
A body without a face.

Your love is my gravity,
I'm walking among the stars.
The only place I wanna be:
Everywhere you are.

At first, I couldn't relate,
As I floated in the void.
How long did I wait
In dark matter absorb?

Your pull is strong
In the realm of dreams
Slowly, I move along
The cosmic stream.

Beyond the horizon
I feel you all around
Everything aligning
Conscience endowed.

All things at one time,
In outer space,
Singularity of mind
A body without a face.

UNDER THE MOONLIGHT

Under the moonlight, you steal the show,
Your charm's like magic, a trick up your sleeve,
I'll never admit it—but you already know.

You flash that grin, and the world's aglow,
It's unfair, really—you make me believe.
Under the moonlight, you steal the show.

You say I'm stubborn, but even so,
Your laugh is a spell I can't quite retrieve
I'll never admit it—but you already know.

We argue in circles; it's all for show,
But somehow, with you, I don't want to leave.
Under the moonlight, you steal the show.

You're trouble, it's true—yet I can't let go,
You've got me hooked, though I play naive.
I'll never admit it—but you already know.

So here I am, and it's quite the blow—
My heart's in your hands; no tricks up my sleeve.
Under the moonlight, you steal the show,
I'll never admit it—but you already know.

BURN IT ALL

How long will you lie to me?
How long will you deceive me?
I told you I would die for you
To show you, I touched the sky for you.
And this is how you treat me.

Was I ever good enough for you?
I lifted you up; you brought me down.
I let you in, and you shut me out.
I can't pretend that love doesn't count,
Even when you are not around.
You were all I would think about.

Hearts don't break until they fall.
I wondered how long it would take
Before our love hit the wall.
And now, I want to burn it all
And watch the ashes fall.
Burn it all down.

In the still of the night,
I hear the echoes of our fights.
But this one was different;
You say I never listen,
Well this time, I'm all ears—

Promises made and broken,
I'm left to pick up the pieces,
Hoping to mend the shattered trust.

BURN IT ALL

I try to find fragments of us
Scattered in the winds,
At each step—a memory
Of where we've been.
Your laughter was my song.
Your smile was my sun.
Without your love to guide me,
This house—it's not a home.
I'd rather watch it burn than linger on.

I wander through shadows
With nowhere to hide
The flames of our past
Burn bright in my mind.
I want to burn it all
And watch the ashes fall.
I want to burn it all down.

At least from the ashes
New beginnings rise,
A future free from deceit and lies.
Through the fire, chastened,
My spirit won't break—
 In the end together, this
Path together we can take.

It's no secret that I'm at my weakest
When you're not around
I want to burn it all—
I want to burn it all down.

A SYMPHONY OF LOVE

In the grand ballroom of Lover's Square,
Where emotions waltz, and temperatures flare,
The heart, a maestro with seduction's wand,
Conducts a symphony of lust until dawn.

Bodies are the dancers, no suits and ties,
Twisting and turning, they lift and rise.
Tenderness whispers sweet nothings in ears.
Cheek to cheek as separation disappears.

The lover's heartbeat, a relentless drum,
Echoes the rhythms of pleasure's soft hum.
Dreams spin in a dimly lit room;
As bodies swim in their perfume.

The temptress' paintbrush strokes are new,
Colors of ecstasy and ebony's hue.
Stars, the audience, they gingerly sit,
Applauding the spectacle of romance's skit.

Murmurs, whisper, soft and sweet,
With fingers caressing from head to feet.
In this dance, bodies move with grace,
Some stumble, some fall, if done in haste.

But the show goes on, and the curtain never falls.
In the theater of love, when passion calls,
Lovers dance fast—then slow, with highs and lows,
To create a masterpiece, this private show♂♀

HEARTACHE

My love is heartache.
The more I let you in,
The more you break.
Your words cut, like a knife,
My heart like a steak.

Your smile brightens my day.
But what takes the sun away
It is your frown.
Meeting you, I swore I found
Heaven on earth,
Someone to build a life with—
Then you left me standing in the dirt.

A hopeless romantic I was.
Your words kept me captivated
Like a moth to a flame.
I soon realized that it was you,
The principal of my pain.

Heartache— say goodbye,
This loneliness won't do.
I now realize no more pain
Means no more you.

And now that we're through,
Now that you're gone,
I won't miss you—
I can breathe again
There's no more pain,
There's no more you.
Don't you get it?

WHAT'S GOOD

Who's the victim of this mistake?
Will it make a difference
If we go our separate ways?
Forgive this, my foolish pride,
What's good about goodbye?

We talk but never listen—
Do you think we should separate?
If leaving makes you cry,
What's good about goodbye?

You say love's in remission;
So, do not resuscitate.
Losing you is a life sentence,
For one foolish mistake.

Am I still heaven-sent
Now that I've gone astray?
We could give it another try,
Or have one last kiss—and let it die.

You said it's forever,
I assume it not too late.
We could do it all together,
Through it all, come what may.
 Let's give it one more try.
If leaving makes you cry,
Then tell me—
What's good about goodbye?

I FOUND YOU

I found a real love.
Now I know the meaning of—
We fit like hand and glove.
Drama in my rear-view,
Now, I only want to focus
On you—on you.

Sparks flew at first sight,
Real love on a one-night.
Reflecting the moonlight,
Enjoying the angelic view
Looking down at you.

Hickeys stain like tattoos,
It used to be a thing,
But now it's so taboo—taboo.
Bodies merge like camouflage,
Kisses get us tongue-tied.

What I didn't know
That is what I never knew.
A real love until found you—
I found you♥

IF THIS IS LOVE

Tell me now, what do you see
When you turn your eyes to me?
Am I the person in your dreams,
Or just a shadow in between?

Do you believe in tales so true,
Where love is pure, and hearts renew?
When the girl finds her perfect guy,
And together, they take to the sky?
But like fireflies, we burn so bright,
Then fade away in the chill of night.

Yet still, my heart can't help but say—
You're the joy that brightens my day.

You're the sunshine breaking through,
A gentle light because of you.
You bring a smile I can't erase,
But you say "friends" and leave no trace.

If this is love, then let it be,
I want it all, just you and me.
If this is love, don't turn away,
I need your warmth and to hear
You sat it—

IF THIS IS LOVE

Time for us: the great divide.
It's time we speak the truth we hide,
Let all these feelings come untied.

A chance you let slip from
Destiny's grasp,
The words from your lips tumble
And crashed.

Don't you see that I still care?
This love we share is always there.
We take to the skies, we burn, we fly,
Yet still, my heart can't say goodbye.
I needed you close; I need your flame
To lose you now would bring me pain.

If this is love, then let it be,
I want it all, just you and me.
If this is love, don't turn away,
I need your warmth and to hear
You say it—

IF I COULD

I'd like to be,
   In your company,
     Sharing your love.

If I could,
   I'd give you the world,
     All that you see,
       Even heaven above.

If I could?
   But I'm just a man in love,
     Someone unworthy of
       The joy you've given me.

Maybe in time, my insecurity
   Would allow me to breathe,
    To believe as you believe,
      That you're all I'll ever need.

For now, so you know,
   My heart melts away like snow
    When you came around.

My defenses were up,
   It was more than enough,
    But you broke them down.

IF I COULD

If I could,
   I'd like to start over.
     Forget about me
        Never opening doors,
           Or pulling out your chair.

I never said ladies first—
   But I always put you first.
     I was always there,

To catch you if you fall.
   Your umbrella in the rain,
     I never miss a call,
        I answered on the first ring.

You say actions speak louder
   Than words, I don't just want
     To Be Heard—
       I want to love you
         Until satisfaction
           And let your words
             Be my action.

GIRL TONIGHT

Girl tonight, your beauty takes flight,
Your love lifts my soul like wings to the air,
Each moment with you feels perfectly right.

The stars lose their shimmer, outshone by your light,
A glow that no other could ever compare.
Girl tonight, your beauty takes flight.

Your laughter, like music, makes darkness feel bright,
A melody sweet beyond all repair.
Each moment with you feels perfectly right.

You bring me to life, turn wrong into right,
With you, every burden is easy to bear.
Girl tonight, your beauty takes flight.

I dream of your touch in the still of the night,
A love that feels endless, beyond any prayer.
Each moment with you feels perfectly right.

Your presence is magic, pure bliss in my sight,
A treasure so rare, so precious, so fair.
Girl tonight, your beauty takes flight,
Each moment with you feels perfectly right.

CHAPTER 2

MINUTES AND MEMORIES

Life is a mosaic of moments—some joyful, some painful, but all undeniably human. In this section, we explore the experiences that connect us across generations, from the exuberance of youth to the reflections of age.

Everyday life is where we find the small, quiet victories that lift our spirits and the inevitable struggles that shape who we are. It's a celebration of the highs and lows that remind us of the resilience of the human spirit and the threads of harmony that tie us together.

PETALS & THORNS

If again this life I could live,
I would spend every waking
Moment smelling the fragrant
Roses—

Plucking each delicate petal one
By one, pricking my fingers on
Its thorns, still I would endeavor to
Hold it.

With eyes wide closed, bring it up
To my nose to savor the sweet smell
Of nectar.

I would use its colors for blush.
My cheeks flushed with life.
Gentle would be my touch.

I would cradle it in my palms,
Watch it grow with love beneath
The sun in the floral garden.

Dance joyfully without shoes,
Swaying with heartfelt gratitude,
Beneath the rain—an enchanted warden.

I valued it more than daffodils,
Cherry Blossom, or poppy fields,
Out numbering the grains of sand.

I'd wade through thorn and
Thistle,
Endure the many prickles,
Just to hold it once again.

Life moves so fast,
Barely enough time to react—
To savor the small doses.

If I could do it all again,
Life would be better spent
Stopping, and smelling the
Roses.

17 FLOORS

I watch from a perch on high,
The bustling life below.
Shadows in Motion collide,
As seen from the 17th floor.

Faces blur as bodies stir
Against the gritty streets below.
Mum's the word, nothing heard
Above the quiet echo.

I wave and smile,
Behave like a child,
Some people stop and stare.
A room within a room,
A reflection within a bloom,
Most pretend that I'm not there.

Daylight, golden and warm,
Radiate through the glass,
I yield to the scintillating sun
For as long as it would last.

Like balloons drifting high
Tethered by memories;
Time slowly passes by
Ever so gently.

17 FLOORS

Sunset blisters across the sky
In orange and velvet hue,
The city slowly comes alive
Neon lights blossom,
Like a cosmic stew.

In the distance, trees,
Some without leaves
Cast shadows across the grass.
My pillow—my silent confidant
Behind this sliver of glass.

From this high place,
The world stretches ever more,
A sprawling cityscape,
With endless secrets to explore.

A view to die for
Above the city's roar,
With dreams on the rise,
All from the seventeenth floor.

MOTHER EARTH

Mother Earth, my guardian,
Rivers once flowed with crystal
Gleam beneath your skies.

Your forests whispered ancient
Dreams mountains kissed the
Heavens high—beneath your
Watchful eye.

Flourishing lands where nature
Thrived, corporations came, and
Balance died.

With ruthless hands, they tore and bled—
To fill their pockets forests shed.
Cattle now graze where jungles fade,
The Amazon's beauty now erased,
The Rainforest lost its natural place
For profit's sake.

They strip your trees; they taint
Your seas; and scar the land. They
Wound your heart; your tears fall
As acid rain, and your cries echo
In vain.

MOTHER EARTH

Beneath the scorching sun's embrace,
   Glaciers melt, and oceans rise,
   Forests burn with fierce, untamed
   Flames that scratch the sky.
   Heedless they are—you weep, and
   You bleed.

O Mother Earth, your children blind,
   To all you give, to all they find.
   Toxic rivers, and wasted cloth,
   Our planet pays a hefty cost.

Before the beauty turns to waste;
Before the oceans are displaced,
And the gifts are lost—let's rise
And renew what men have frayed.

Together, before the sky vanquishes,
Before we seed to greed our powers,
Let's rise and be unafraid to take
Back what is ours?

HAPPY HOUR

I think about things
   That makes me giggle,
     Even just a little,
        And my funny bone tickles.

From my throat, like bubbles,
   As simple as a chuckle,
     I laugh out loud
        Though standing in a crowd.

For air, I would grasp
   Depending on the laugh
      And how long it would last.
     Inside jokes are
       Like laughing gas.

Tears pool in my eyes,
   Head thrown back,
     I slap my thigh,
       Rock back and forth,
       Sometimes I snort.

Laughter's like a fizzy drink,
   It makes me blush and think,
     Gives me hiccups, I even cry,
     So I never laugh and drive.

I smile to pay a happy toll,
   A bite of joy for every soul.
     So why laugh with moderation
      When joy is a path less taken?

Laugh away, don't hold back.
   It's okay to go on a giggling spree.
    It's life's best little hack, so relax,
     Sit down have a laugh: On me.

SUNSHINE & JOY

I remember being a kid
And the silly things I did,
Like pretending to run away,
But I ended up in the park,
Where children would play.
We'd laugh and shout all day.

We mounted swings that would
Fly, we sent kites up high;
Our joy colored the sky
In a beautiful array—

We swarm the playground,
And our laughter would soar.
We would swing, climb, and roar,
On slides slick, played games
Quick as a flick,
Which made us clamor evermore.

I loved those bright, sunny days.
We were able to laugh and play,
Run and jump in a big grassy
Clump until night chased
The sunlight away.

TIN ROOF

I would like to propose a toast—

From humble beginnings,
To life in the city.
Here's to "never go back".
If the truth be told
I was an unfortunate soul
To have grown up in a shack.

The roof made of tin,
It rattled in the wind,
Banged every time it stormed.
Floorboards squeaked
The faucet always leaked
It was better than living in a barn.

A shack on a plot of land
My clothing was secondhand
We were poor, and I never knew.
Barely had running water
An outhouse for a toilet
Raindrops seep from the roof.

My father was a sharecropper,
He drank whiskey from the bottom,
He spent most of his time at the bar,
Singing songs by Muddy Waters,
Dressed like a squatter,
Strumming on his old guitar.

TIN ROOF

He worked like a slave,
Barely got paid,
With three mouths to feed.
He dreamed of being a star,
But he never got far
So, he decided to leave.

He packed up his clothes,
Walked out the front door,
Never once did he look back.
Speed off in his truck,
An old black pickup
Called "Hit The Road Jack".

I never heard from my father
No message in the bottle
No Postcard telling us where he was at.
Life got much harder
The minimum wage was a dollar
Mom worked herself to death.

I will never forget
How the raindrops hit
That old tin roof. " Ra-Ta-Ta-Ta"
From humble beginnings
To life in the city
Here's to "never going back."

IF NOT ME

I wouldn't want to be a dog that chases a cat.
Or a cat chasing a rat, nor would I want to be,
As blind as a bat.

Not a icky fly nibbling on every icky thing it sees
Not a bird with the ability to glide, as a chick,
Very few survive.

Or bouncy as a bumblebee Surfing a breeze
Sucking on honeydew thick and sweet,
Buoyant as a Whale riffling the sea,
Fins-like cells to carry me.

How about a worm burrowing through the muck,
Not afraid of getting stuck, but If I couldn't
See the sun, I would miss it too much.

I prefer to be a caterpillar, nibbling on a leaf,
Or a squirrel climbing a tall tree. A caterpillar—
That's what I want to be: nimble and long
Able to reach, then float as a butterfly
Light as a feather beneath a blue sky
Enjoying the weather.

Or—an Amoeba as small as can be.
That way, no one would notice me,
As I live out my days in secrecy.
If I could be anything else but me—
What should I be?

BITTER TEARS

I sit on the porch as the sun dips low,
Strumming my guitar soft and slow.
Dreaming of the days when I was young,
Life was then simple—now a bygone.

Now, these bitter tears do fall,
Under moonlight's tender call.
Thoughts of days when joy ran high,
Day or night, time would fly.

Dirt road winds where memories bloom,
Past fields where I danced in tune.
The echoes of laughter fade—
A time I loved, but life betrayed.
These fond memories are surviving friends.

In this place, long nights bend.
Each tear burns with a bitter flame,
A time lost, I can't reclaim.
Still, these bitter tears do fall,
Under moonlight's tender call.

I long for the days when joy ran high,
Back when youth was mine, time would fly.
Beneath the stars, I wish for it again,
The constant aches of a grumpy old man,
Who often burns with mortal desire,
Reminiscing only stokes the fire.

I'M HOME

I lay beneath a blanket sky
Monarchs dance below the trees.
Lazy clouds drift way up high
Carried by a gentle breeze.

I love the scent of apple pie
Lemon drops bitter-sweet
That old mare I used to ride
Squishy mud beneath my feet,
It's summertime, and I'm home.

Children play with such joy
Curiosity running wild
Adorn with all the little spoils
That makes one a child.

Fireflies invade the night
Some move like falling stars
The country life, no city lights
Dusty roads and fewer cars,
It's summertime, and I'm home.

In slumber, I hear the rooster crow
"Cock-a-doodle-do"
I often wonder how does
The rooster know when to
"Cock-a-doodle-do"

I'M HOME

Bouncy sprite to life, I clamor
Thrusting wide the shutters
Just outside, I see grandma Nana
Missy the cow and mother
It's summertime, and I'm home.

ANYWHERE BUT HERE

Facing a starlit space,
Dreams whisper of distant shores,
Where the sky and the sea embrace,
Where freedom's wind forever roars.

Mountains rise beyond the haze,
Climbing peaks of lofty heights
Valleys where the sunlight plays,
Chasing shadows into night.

Forests deep with ancient trees,
Whisper tales of time gone by,
Rivers sing with melodies,
Underneath a northern sky.

Cities sparkle in the dark,
Lights that dance like stars above,
Every valley, every park,
It tells a story of joy and love.

Deserts vast and oceans wide,
Trails that lead to worlds unknown,
With each step and every stride,
A feeling, the urge, the need to roam.

To hear the world's unspoken song,
To find peace of mind.

CHAPTER 3

BEYOND THE VEIL

Faith is a bridge—sometimes steady, sometimes fragile—that carries us through life's uncertainties. In this section, I explore the role of religion and spirituality as both a sanctuary and a source of introspection. These poems are reflections on the struggles and triumphs of belief, the questions we dare to ask, and the solace we seek in something greater than ourselves.

Whether grounded in tradition or born from personal exploration, faith is a deeply human experience—both an anchor in the storm and a flicker of light in the dark. Here, you'll find verses that wrestle with doubt, celebrate devotion, and uncover the sacred in the everyday.

This section is for anyone who has ever searched for meaning in the divine, found strength in prayer, or sought peace in the unknown.

FEAITH ENDURES

Each day, I pray beneath
A gray sky as the wealthy
Flaunt gold, their laughter,
A knife.
Another day in shadows.
Dreams dismembered,
My prayer is a solitary fight.

I give to the poor,
With hands worn thin,
Until what is, is no more,
A void deep within.

Each coin a tear, each meal,
A silent hymn, my charity,
Echoes in the wind.

The sun's warmth mingles
With the cold of despair,
Good and evil, an odd pair,
So different, yet the same.
In life's cruel snare,
Shadows softly glare.

FEAITH ENDURES

The rich taunt, like mirages in
The sand.
The haves flaunt and mock my
Empty hands.

My faith remains strong
Through trials, a bright beacon
Like the old spiritual Songs
At times when the flesh weakens.

In the darkest times
My spirit holds true
My unwavering faith
Sees me through.

Each step is a journey
Through twilight's shroud;
Hope's voice is barely loud.
In the quiet, a heart beats,
Defiant and proud,
My struggle is a light beneath
The clouds.

MY GUARDIAN

With wings of light, your whispers
In the breeze, I hear,
In shadows deep or brightest day,
You guide me through the poppy fields.

In silent prayers and candle's glow,
In the songs that every sunrise sings,
Holding back the storms that blow,
With grace unseen, you spread your wings.

With gratitude, my soul does sing,
In laughter, tears, and silent cries,
Each step I take, side by side,
Through life's journey, stride for stride.

In moments when the world feels cold,
For all the hope your presence brings,
You wrap me in your wings to hold;
My heart is whole, and my spirit sings.

In quiet moments, I reflect on blessings
That I can't neglect. With every breath
And whispered prayer, I'm not surprised
To find you there.

Your wings that shelter, eyes that see,
The deepest parts of life and me.
My guardian, you're always here
In my trials and joys shared.

BROKEN WINGS

A dragon's tail, a dragon fell,
A third of heaven's host ensnared.

O scarlet wings of heaven's might,
There, wounded in flight.

From afar, the lattice of your star,
Seen gliding in the night.

Once an angel of light, now halo blight,
In thy heart, evil unfurled.

No longer bright as an angel of light,
But now, downward hurled.

PHANTOM WHISPERS

Phantom whispers and moans,
On a throne of bones,
In a place so dark and desolate.

Black as pitch, inscrutable,
Dreadful yet beautiful,
Home to the malevolent.

Bony fingers creep,
Shadows deep, invading sleep,
Nightmares haunt the dark—

Ghosts without sheets,
Strain my breath in deep retreat,
Paralyzing the heart.

Serrated teeth gleam,
Silent screams in a dream,
Heart beating like a drum.

Mounds of corpses and skulls,
Shadows patrol the cold,
Never to see the sun.

In the night, it creeps,
Of rotten meat, it reeks,
Death's cold, gripping hand.
Savory and sweet,
For treats, it eats,
The soul of every man.

LOVE IMMORTAL

A crescendo of cries penetrate
The sky, beneath the pale radiant
Moon.

Shadows drape the sloppy lawn.
Pillows of immortal icons,
Adorn the many tombs.

Beneath the sod decays the mortal
Heart, family, and friends bereaved.

Oh, vibrant souls of sorrow great,
Soon to share this gloomy fate,
Love alone can we reprieve.

It thrives in the heart and mind,
Comfort to all left behind,
Until that day, a passerby—

To all who find this poem to read,
Death is a finality we all achieve,
But love will never die.

    So let us remember,
    Breathe and smile ☺

ETERNAL TRUST

From the Perils of the world, O Lord
    Keep me close to your heart,
        As I bear my burdens
        In the heat of the day.

My Savior, beloved,
    Let me exhale in judgment's hour,
        Finding shelter in the arms of grace.

When the last trumpet sounds,
    Suffer not your word abound
    To tumble or fall.
        As men wicked spawn
            Stand before Your throne,
            Both great and small.

Within Your tender care,
    My soul laid bare,
        Cradled in Your arms.

A healing power
    At that faithful hour,
        Forgiveness will feel like a balm.
        Through trials faced,
            In Your embrace,
                Strength in each endeavor.

With angels, I'll sing
    Before my Lord, my King,
        And dwell with You forever.

CYCLE OF LIFE

People are yet born, hoping to elude death,
No existing love spawns from our unprotected
Self.

We live, and we die upon this earthly sphere,
Joy and pain we cry, the unknown we fear.

Children frolic with vigor, all the purity of youth,
But if the aged can, and if the youth only
Know.

Etched in stone our fate, old become the new,
All who reawaken experience déjà vu.

Tomorrow is sooner gone, like clouds, a passerby,
In reality, we are pawns of the watchers on high.

Mortality will lay bare foolish dreams of forever,
We live in despair, invisible strings a tether.

The illusion is life, a momentary break,
From the eternal night, from which we awake.

Mystery guides our steps, bittersweet and brief,
In the arms of death, we slept and will sleep.

GOD'S SIGNATURE

Upon these heavens, our ancestors gazed,
Dazzled by beauty in midnight's embrace,
Stars like jewels in the dark, unfazed,
Echoing mysteries of the cosmic space.

A crystal tapestry where wonders dwell,
Their chorus sang long before our birth,
A testament of God that stories tell,
Uniting both the heavens and the earth.

They witnessed Lucifer's fall from grace,
Saw Cain's dark deeds in shadows cast,
Twinkled at Calvary, in that solemn place,
Where gentle Christ breathed his last.

For countless years, they've shone so bright,
Undimmed in grandeur through the ages,
Gems of the sky, celestial light,
Writing the divine in cosmic pages.

From infancy, we sense the great unknown,
More than meets the eye, the stars convey,
A signature of God, eternally shown,
Written in the skies, guiding our way.

REFLECTIONS

In love's gentle cradle,
Whispers of peace,
The heart finds joy
In the bitter-sweet—
In the loss, we confront
Shadows so deep,
Yet hope remains
In memories we keep.

Faith lights the path
Through utter despair,
A beacon of strength,
Only the faithful share.
Battling seas of moral plight,
With hands locking hands,
With courage and unity,
Together, we stand.

Each prayer is a reflection,
A glimpse into the soul,
Through love, loss, and faith,
We become whole.
Some things we challenge,
With unwavering might,
A journey of healing to the
World, a light.

EDEN'S FIRST TALE

In Eden's garden, pure and bright,
Lived Adam and Eve in pure delight.
They roamed with grace before the fall
Among the flora and fauna's call.

There, beneath the green canopy,
Wade the unsuspecting Eve,
Plucking cherries from the cherry tree,
In grassy weeds below the knees.

Lurking in the shadows of the thicket, hushed
A serpent in the garden lay,
Curled about a mulberry bush,
Sheltered from the light of day.

His disdain for heaven knew no bounds,
It had been waiting forever to tarnish the Crown.
In shadows deep through whispers sly,
To lead men from the light awry,
The Serpent weaves a cunning plan,
With a forked tongue and hidden guise,
To spark the fall of precious man.

From the boughs of his parasol,
He came crawling like a wheel
Within a wheel, uncoiling.

EDEN'S FIRST TALE

"Eve!" he hissed,
Weaving through the grassy-tall.
He spoke each word with a lisp,
And "Eve!" he still called.

Dig if you will, Eve with her finger still,
Twisting a lock of hair,
Supple brown skin, completely bare,
Leaning against the cherry tree.

The Serpent whispered in her ear quietly,
So, as none could overhear,
Eve listening and thinking,
Thinking still.

Adam on leisure or task of crown
None the wiser—nowhere to be found.

In the balance, all of creation hung,
If Eve could only temptation shun.
Alas, the Serpent, as cunning as its deed,
Beguiled poor Eve and all of paradise
Bereaved.

MY SAVING GRACE

My world was dark,
And shadows loomed
Grace gently came,
Dispelling all my gloom,
A whisper-sweet that
Led me through the fray.

Drowning in my sins,
Lost and so consumed,
My spirit is now whole
With faith renewed
In pain and hurt,
My Lord found a way.

Because of faith,
There's heaven up above,
Where Lord and King
Turn night into the brightest day.
One day, I'll see the
Face, that light of love,

Through trials faced,
My eyes upon the goal,
With heart in peace,
Forever, I will stay.
Grace came to save
And heal my weary soul.

CHAPTER 4

FIGHT FOR TOMORROW

This chapter explores the journey of rising above adversity—fighting for equality. These poems reflect the struggles faced, the dreams pursued, and the victories achieved. They honor survival and protest but also celebrate the boundless contributions of Black communities to art, culture, science, and the world at large.

Above all, these Poems are a tribute to the enduring spirit of hope—reminding us that even in struggle, there is beauty, and in unity, there is power. Healing begins when we listen, confront hard truths, and commit to the work of change. Let these Poems be both a reflection and a call to action—a reminder of where we've been, where we are, and where we must go, as well as the importance of getting there together.

BLACK SWAN

Where are the black heroes?
Can someone let them know,
We need you—

To be our guide or muse.
To whom should we aspire,
If not, you?

Antihero, "Black swan",
Are you not born
A burdensome color?

Black and despised,
Told to take pride
In a life of struggles.

Haven't you drunk your fill?
No elixir of a sort can quell,
The unbearable truth.

Generations live in despair.
Caught up in the snares,
Of youth—

BLACK SWAN

From Whom do we take
Our queue,
Our marching orders,
If not, you?

If not now, then when?
If not today, how then
Can a better tomorrow
Dawn?

Like reefs bending in the wind
We hold on to kith and kin
Waiting for your return.

Emerge from your cocoon,
Sip from destiny's spoon,
Stand in shadows place.

Give the marching orders
Inspire, and we will follow
For you, we are ready,
We wait.
We need you!

BROWN FACE

Brown face, I see your grace—
The beauty in your complexion.
I love the way you celebrate
The richness of your essence,

Brown face, Rich and warm,
Like autumn's shades, you shine,
As the sun dances off your skin
With melanin to protect you.

Among many colors and hues,
Heaven has made you uniquely
Beautiful.

With eyes that gleam—In you,
I see the threads of history,
A masterpiece crafted—the potter's
Clay.

Brown face, you are the song;
"A Melody of Beauty".
Wear it with pride—for I can see
Why others stare with envy.

You age gracefully beneath
The sky—your beauty dances,
In sunlight's warmth,
You glow in every direction.
Such a beautiful complexion ☺

THE EAGLE SOARS

Ebony souls meander,
Across the African plains,
Bought and sold their weight
In gold—Branded, shackled,
And Chained.

The cracking of the whip,
Gnashing of teeth.
In the bowls of rickety ship,
Kith and kin are bereaved.

America adorned her infant shores,
With treasures of all sorts;
Blacksmiths, healers, farmers,
Sojourned her rigid ports.

For greed—for all the glory
She would suffer no defeat.
Far removed from piety,
Sunk her talents deep.

Even now, the eagle soars,
On the backs of the poor.
Their stories written in scars,
A testament to who they are.

We remember their sacrifice
And honor the many lives she stole.
Together, we rise, we soar,
With courage and hope forevermore.

BLACK EXCELLENCE

From ancient sands to modern lands,
Black hands have shaped the earth.
They've shown their boundless worth,
In science, art, and medicine's birth.

Art flows in veins, pure and true
Basquiat's strokes are vibrant and blue.
Baldwin's words, a symphony of thought,
Each line a lesson the soul has sought.

Music's heartbeat echoes the soul,
From jazz to blues, rock and roll.
Nina Simone's voice, a clarion call,
Resonating deep in gilded halls.

Inventors, with minds alight,
Garrett Morgan's life-saving traffic light.
Mark Dean's vision, a world made new,
Shaping computers we all use,
With patents, bold, and breakthroughs.

In literature, we write our truth—
Maya Angelou's words, are a fountain of youth.
Her pen sang freedom, her spirit soared,
A legacy—a treasure adored.

BLACK EXCELLENCE

In every field, our light gleams,
A legacy of hope, a timeless beam.
Black excellence—a profound force,
In every corner of the world, a voice.

BLACK FACE

Behind the mask, a hollow gaze,
A soul looms in the shadow's maze.
Eyes shimmer, cold and stark,
A heart eclipsed, lost in the dark.

Blackface, a crude disguise,
Exposes the void they tried to hide.
The mask, a fortress, makes them bold,
Yet, fail to hide the darker soul.

When Faces are painted black
   A vial heart is shown
      A mask is donned—
         To stoke fear,
            To silence the pride,
               To humble the chosen,
                  But we rise.

A mask of hate, both bold and shy,
A morally bankrupt soul it hides.
In the balance of conceal and rant,
A paradox grim, citizens dance
Behind the shield—pale eyes loom.

A reflection of the broken soul,
The private tales it grooms,
A history of barbarity, they perpetrate
In disguise, with painted faces ☻

THE STIGMA

Eyes that judge, mock, and revile,
Those "half-devil and half-child,"

View our blackness with disdain,
The stigma clings as a sooted shroud.
Yet we rise from the ash of history,
With a spirit, unapologetic-ally proud.

We are the moral chrysalis,
The dreams that refuse to die.
For hope, we are the catalyst,
Held down yet 'still we rise.'

We are the children of the sun
Unlike fauna running wild
Beneath the sun—bodies burn
Those "half-devil and half-child."

So let them stare with envy
The beauty is in the face,
The strength in the eyes,
Skin adorned with grace.

The stigma of blackness,
Thought to weigh us down,
Yet, our spirit remains unbroken,
Abased, but now abound.

GREED OF THE MAN

He comes to the hood
To take what is good.
All else is left to neglect.
Tell this one, and that
"You're an exceptional Black,
Better than all the rest."

He feeds the starved dignity
Of those who dream of fame.
They find their place in history;
Their wealth—the grifter drains.

His watchful eye spies
As he picks and chooses.
Victims of his heart's desire
Are those easily fooled.

Words from his mouth.
With a straight face,
Crooked neck,
He negotiates the cost

"Your culture, of course."
"Your style, your dance,
I'll take that too."
"Your history, your victories,
I'll put that to good use."
"Humility or divinity,
Whatever makes you, you."

"Your rhythm but not your blues."
"Your break-dance, moonwalk,
Though I could never walk
In your shoes." I want it all."

"You are to the world—a muse."
"What say I grant in return
To oblige me with this ruse?"
"If you say all this I've earned,
Things I'll give to you in return:"

With a straight face,
Crooked neck,
Unfold his double tongue.

"I'll let you bask in the sun,
Sip from the dew of dawn,
Dance on the air that blows."
"Now I know—
God to all have given this free."
"But as far as you're concerned,
God, too, belongs to me."

IN THE GHETTO

Streets are tared with pain—
A concrete maze of endless strain,
Silent cries and broken dreams,
Hope is scarce, or so it seems.

Face and hands are bloody-stained
An oppressive system at play.
Bodies trapped in mental chains,
From which few ever escape.

Sirens squeal across polluted air,
Whispering tales of deep despair.
Blue and red lights, a constant sight,
You can hardly say it is fair.

Children play with innocent hearts,
They dance before the beast.
Parade about like jovial larks,
In shadows where strangers creep.

Many pay the cost of hustle to survive.
Young souls lost—some buried alive.
Graffiti walls and vacant lots mark
The struggles and battles fought.

IN THE GHETTO

In the ghetto—
Every day, hope departs.
Silent halls and hollow hearts,
Here, the walls close in tight,
Dirty, cold, and devoid of light.

Streets paved with pain,
A morbid beast to tame—
Muted songs where crowds belong.
In concrete cages, dreams are confined,
In this place, behind invisible lines,
There is no peace of mind—

RICH EAT POOR

In the land of opportunity,
Home to the golden chains,
Where Freedom wears a price tag,
The wealthy dance, a masquerade,
Getting riches from toil and pain.

In Fortune's game, we place our bets
On dreams spun from silver nets,
A pyramid built on shifting sand,
A house of cards in a trembling
Hand.
Coins whisper secrets in the night,
Promises of fleeting delight,
Yet wealth, a ghost, slips away;
Beyond the gilded cage, we stay.

Golden chains clink—
Glittering but tight,
Shackles restrain the feet —
No escaping this gloomy plight.

The clock ticks—time a silent thief,
As profit's tunes brings no relief.
Cha-ching—the balance tips, a careful art,
In this grand bazaar, we play our part.

RICH EAT POOR

Behind the curtain, strings pulled,
In this theater, dreams are sold,
Masked in gold, the players sway,
While shadows deal with the cards
We play♠

Golden chains bind wrists and minds,
Freedom, an illusion, they find.
Bound by wealth yet seeking more,
In this game of rich eating poor.

A COLONY

Enslaved, in rage,
    Hands up, hands out.
        Face down on the
        Pavement.

From desegregation
    To welfare plantation,
        Cites of black faces.

On both knees— can't breathe,
    No justice, It's just us.
        And a starved sense of dignity.

Others bore the stripes,
    Now, we fight for our rights,
        Ancestors, now progeny.

Arrested development
    Arrested for the hell of it
        Blue lights in the rear-view.

Black reality,
    Police brutality
        Another life code blue.

Souls of the restless,
    Labeled as miss-fits
        Detained in the Ghettos.

A COLONY

Voter suppression
   Limited protection
      It's Jim Crow 2.0.

Son like father
   Born to be fodder
      Fuel for the system.

No money for college
   Deprived of knowledge.
      In most families, a schism.

Soulless deprived
   White-face disguised
      We grapple for liberation.

Black and despised
   Attacked from all sides
      A colony within a nation.

SLAVE PROGENY

I am indeed a descendant of slaves
Once bought and sold as beasts,
For several hundred years,
My ancestors' labored without cease.

Born black and despised,
They toiled without God or law
To inveigh against the vile nature
Of those devoid of benevolence.

My own experiences border this reality,
The parasitic nature of a colonizer.
Acts of moral turpitude afflicting lives
Without hope or reprisal.

I dare to imagine slavery's extremes,
When men despised morality to feed
Their greed.
Millions cried for justice—but found none.
Only the cold, damp earth to encapsulate
Their decaying corpses.

SLAVE PROGENY

America has never shown pity,
For the "Salve progenies."
For the crowded cities
For the "light-skinned
Or mahogany—

For the souls of a horrid past.
To ensure none suffered in vain.
So let us put "This System" to task,
Force "The winds of change."

Born black, thrust into the struggle,
What does it mean to be free,
A father, brother, sister or mother
To be us, to be you—me?

The "Slave Progeny.

DEMOCRACY?

In the land of the free,
Dreams are sold,
It is a tale of democracy,
A story old.

In the land where freedom
Rings,
Faith in democracy sings.
Yet beneath the anthem's
Guise, all lies.

Money whispers in the lofty
Halls,
The puppet Sits behind oval
Walls.
We, the people, are bribed.

In the land where freedom's
Flag is hung,
A tale of democracy forever
Young.

Yet, in the pages of our founding
Creed,
It's a word we are yet to read.
"Democracy" is a fallacy, fools
Gold.
A dream detached from reality,
It's the greatest lie ever told.

THIS OLD THING

Dust stirs, scattered by the winds,
Settling in unseen and forgotten places.
Leaves, twist—tossed, never to rejoin
The tree again.
Their stories carry beyond branches.

Brothers, strangers with familiar blood,
A puzzle is missing its frame.
No father—only the mother's love,
Her shadow stretched like a river,
Flowing back from whence it came.

Timeless love—vessels of earth,
Elders blood—a blessing or curse,
Out into the open.
Every current, every twist and turn,
I respawn; I never quit.
Each path leads back to this—to me.

Under the night's heavy black sheet,
Pierced by a million silent pinholes,
They hunt the shadows of the past.
The Patriarchs whisper secretly,

Their voices flow through my veins,
Their strength surges in my chest.
This old thing, this ancient weight,
This inheritance of dust and blood,
They hum, alive within me, my body.
"This Old Thing ".

I WAS THERE

I was there when the first slaves arrived,
In the body of a stranger, I had never met.
Because I am, he yet survives.
Through me, his spirit speaks,
And because he is, that assures my victory.
I was there, and I remember— Because
The struggle, up until this day, continues.

I was there for the march on DC,
The 28th of August 1963.
There were a great many black faces;
Standing beside me.

I was there when the preacher preached,
To keep the peace, we knelt before the beast,
Ignoring the fangs and ferocious teeth,
Of German Dogs—
Terrors of the holocaust used against us,
Fighting not for reparations,
But for the integration of schools
Where teachers would only teach lies
While the truth they would hide
From us.
I was there in 1965, the "Watts Riots."
When police beat black bodies,
When their voices cried out for peace.
Today, their pain lives on in me,
Now, a million blackbirds In my family tree.

I WAS THERE

I was there beneath the flames.
When the protest turned ugly,
When the military occupied
The Streets—1992.

I was there when hope
Loomed beyond reach.
There with you,
Each one locking arms,
We stood in the breach,
As Justice collapsed beneath
The weight of injustice.

A veil as thin as a sheet,
Beneath which Lady Liberty
And hypocrisy sleep.

For years—we have fed
The fragile pride
Of a racist nation where
Only the rich thrive—

"Hands-up, don't shoot,"
Was nothing more than a salute
To deputized assassins—

I was I-was-there.

NO ESCAPING THE PAST

I dreamt I was a fierce warrior
Crossing the African plains,
 Slumped beneath the weight
Of rusty chains.
These dreams are strange,
Enslaved and free—

Young among the captives,
Black bodies carried away,
From Mother Africa
Down the arid steppes of vast,
Beautiful lands.
The smell of the Savannah fades,
The sun bleeds into twilight,
Sinking deeper beneath each wave
Into the darkest of the night.

Dreams and nightmares,
Overlapping like spider-webs
I awake to a cold sweat.
From my window, reality glares,
A dim and hopeless stare.
My life is a hard reset.

There's no escaping the past
The dye, cast—
Caught like fish in the net.
The part I play, free or enslaved,
A result of cause-and-effect.

ENDNOTE

Thank you for walking with me through the spaces in between the moments where love lingers, hurt transforms, and hope quietly rebuilds.

Each poem in these pages holds a piece of my heart, shaped by the bittersweet rhythms of life.
It's my deepest wish that these words have touched you, stirred you, or perhaps reminded you of your own strength and grace.

This journey is ours now, shared in the way only poetry can unite us.

With gratitude and love,

Donald K Bingham

ABOUT THE AUTHOR

Donald K. Bingham is a poet and storyteller whose work delves into the universal emotions that define the human experience. Through themes of love, loss, social justice, and self-reflection, Donald crafts poetry that resonates deeply, offering readers a mirror to their own joys and struggles.

With *Everything In Between*, Donald invites readers to explore the threads that bind us all—those moments of tenderness, resilience, and shared understanding.

When he's not writing, Donald enjoys reading, creating music, video game design and uncovering inspiration in life's unexpected twists—both its triumphs and its disappointments. This compilation reflects that journey, written with the hope of sparking reflection, unity, and a deeper appreciation for the world around us.